# My Barbie Was an Amputee
And Other Essays

# My Barbie Was an Amputee
## And Other Essays

*Angie Vicars*

Celtic Cat Publishing
Knoxville, Tennessee

Published by Celtic Cat Publishing
Knoxville, Tennessee
www.celticcatpublishing.com

Acknowledgements: Special thanks to Linda Parsons Marion for graciously providing guidance, the critical eye, and deft touch. The author also is grateful to the editors of Metro Pulse, a Knoxville weekly which first published, in their original form, the essays contained in this collection.

Manufactured in the United States of America
Design by Dariel Mayer
Cover photographs by Kate Ogle

ISBN: 0-9658950-7-6
Library of Congress Control Number: 2005938854

Also by Angie Vicars:
*Treat* (a novel), The Haworth Press Inc., 2001

# Contents

# Preface and Dedication

I was going to say that this collection of essays started in high school when my creative writing teacher, Bobbi Range, told me that I was a born essayist.

However, the truth is that I started telling stories before I could write. I have to thank my family for introducing me to the storytelling tradition. My father told stories to my brother and me when we were ready to go to sleep. My mother told stories about her family.

I started my story-telling career with a tape recorder and a microphone that my brother got for a Christmas present. Whenever he wasn't using them, I was. I once found a battered cassette tape on which my brother says, "Tell us a story, possum." Then a voice begins that I didn't even recognize because it sounded so much like a cartoon character on helium. It was me rattling off a story about my stuffed dog, Blue.

By elementary school, I was a playwright-in-the-making. Unfortunately, I cast so many of my classmates that there was hardly anyone left to watch the show. I think my first effort was called "The Court Trial that Failed."

At high school, I wrote an essay about the only Barbie I ever owned and the tragic turn of events that left her one leg short. A reworked version of that essay was the first piece of freelance writing that I had published—admittedly for no pay

—but it was so good seeing my name in print. That essay is the first essay in this book and the inspiration for the title.

From 1995 through 2003, many of the essays that comprise this collection made their initial appearances in Metro Pulse, Knoxville's weekly paper. They sometimes ran under a column called Yikes that was perfect for my habits as well as my interests. Many thanks to the Pulse for not only proving my English teacher right but, more importantly, for turning it into a paying gig.

I also wish to thank my dear friend Julie Auer, who not only appointed herself my agent for this project, but who insists on working for a bottle of wine. At least she does for me, the rest of you have to negotiate.

Most of all, thank you Kate, a gifted artist in your own right. Your belief in me brought this collection into print and assures me that I'll always have plenty more to say.

# My Barbie Was an Amputee
And Other Essays

# My Barbie Was an Amputee

Yes, this story is gruesome . . . but true. I should've been satisfied with my GI Joe and Johnny West dolls, but no. I wanted more. All the other girls I knew had Barbies, so I wanted one too. And I didn't just want Barbie the doll. I had big dreams. I wanted a Barbie carry case filled with a Barbie wardrobe. I wanted a Barbie townhouse, a Barbie Ultravette, even a Barbie pool. I wanted to be part of the crowd, the cool girls, and the girls who played with Barbies.

If only I had foreseen the tragedy that awaited, I'd never have selected Malibu Barbie from her synthetic sand-and-sea Sears catalog background. I'd have waited until the idea of bendable-leg Barbies was only a dim memory in some former Mattel executive's mind. But on that Christmas morning when I unwrapped Barbie's box, all I could see was nine inches of deeply tanned perfection smiling winningly at me through the cellophane.

Out of the box, it was a different story. I have to admit it. Barbie kind of caught me by surprise—not because of her lack of anatomy or the fact that her fingers were molded together. GI Joe and Johnny West suffered from those maladies too (well, there was that GI Joe with the Kung Fu grip, but even he hadn't been designed with opposable thumbs that worked.)

What surprised me about Barbie was that her feet were arched. I'd never had a doll who was permanently standing on tiptoe before. How was she supposed to wear sneakers like Skipper? And I couldn't get another outfit on her to save my life. Her rubber limbs (we're talking the '70s here, okay?) were like glue. I pulled and yanked to the ruin of my little fingernails, but succeeded only in getting her pants to her knees where they stuck hard and fast.

I couldn't show her to my friends like this. She was mooning everyone. What was so great about Barbie after all, I wondered? I decided to put the townhouse request on hold temporarily. First, I wanted to see how sturdy she was.

Not very, I soon discovered. The first time I took Barbie skiing (in our hallway mounted on the slope of one of the Partridge Family albums), she broke her leg. Lying there with her white plastic socket showing through a split in her previously perfect skin, she looked as human as I'd ever seen her.

But that wasn't the point. She was Barbie. She wasn't supposed to look human. She was supposed to look better. Not only was she flawed now, but I still couldn't get any pants on her. The cool girls would laugh at me. This wasn't my dream. This was a nightmare. Only five years old, I already felt cheated by corporate America.

At this point my brother stepped in. He claimed to be the world's finest Barbie surgeon, and offered to see what he could do. A few minutes later, he handed Barbie back to me with masking tape wound around her leg from top to bottom. I handed her right back. "I can't take her out like this. All she can wear is that bathing suit. Everyone will see her leg. No one will play with me. That's un . . . that's un . . . that's no good." After a quick argument over the fact that GI Joe would be proud to wear a cast, he offered me another alternative, amputation. "No, are you crazy? She can't just have one leg. She's Barbie." He pointed out that with only one knee maybe I could finally get her pants on. I still held back. Amputation for Barbie?

It just didn't seem right. "Look, would you rather her leg falls off when she's on a date with Ken?"

We went through with the amputation. Well, my brother went through with it. I covered my face with my hands, peeking through my fingers from time to time. I did find I could finally get her pants all the way up to her waist when it was over. But staring at her while she lay in recovery in her tapestried pink and silver "casual threads," that seemed like a small consolation.

This doll was still Barbie, I told myself. Her blue-as-the-bathroom-floor eyes never dimmed. Her "I'm not wearing a bra" smile never disappeared. Yet as I propelled her, with one side of her "disco duds" hanging empty, across the linoleum dance floor in the kitchen I felt cheated. My dream come true wasn't a perfect doll anymore, if she ever had been.

I packed Barbie up in her carry case and put her wardrobe away. Sure, I could've asked for that Ultravette or the Barbie horse and riding outfit. Yet I knew in my heart that these modes of transportation would've helped her, and not me.

I just couldn't deal with it, the death of perfection, the loss of innocence, the row of extra pumps. Looking back on it all, I think Barbie really served as a good introduction to life in the real world. Yes, I was a jaded kindergartener, but I was wiser too. I had my first proof that what you hear about isn't always what you get; that the in-crowd may not be onto anything, and that if you need Vaseline to get your clothes on you may be succumbing to society's pressures a little too much.

As for today's kids, I don't know how they'll learn these valuable lessons. Barbie's gone plastic, and her legs don't bend anymore. She looks less real than ever, but her molded smile stretches so wide I swear I'm going to buy her again someday just so I can black out her teeth.

## Beanie Baby

The Spot (a bar in West Knoxville) is noisy, late on a Friday night. Heather is asking me something for the third time. I see her lips moving. "Wah wah, wah wah wah wah."

"What?" I ask again.

She leans closer, takes a drag on her cigarette and blows the smoke upwards. "I said, are you having a good time?"

"Well . . . "

"Do you want another beer?"

"No," I say so quickly it startles Heather.

It's time to tell the truth. I rarely drink beer anymore, rarely go to bars, am apparently too deaf to hear over live music past a certain decibel level, and find myself craving desserts more often than fries and onion rings.

Over the last few years, my identity has changed. I just don't mix with the drinkers like I used to. Something stirred me, woke me up to my place in the daily grind. That something is coffee. I have become a java head. Pour me another one, Joe. Make it a double.

I wish I could say this was an obvious choice for me, but sometimes, true love must come looking for us. Until the night I fell under the spell of the bean, I had experienced only the grounds of rejection. My stolen sips were bitter, cold, spat in the sink when no one was looking.

It took Deanna to turn my taste. She inched my inhibitions down with platefuls of pasta and multiple Merlots. In the middle of a sentence, I slipped right out of consciousness. That's when she opened my eyes. She was right in front of me with a huge mug of hazelnut, the sugar bowl, the canister of cream, free refills. I had to try. By the next morning, I was in love and java was her name. Oh.

The thing is I wanted to be a beer drinker. When I moved to Knoxville (in the late '80s) and scanned the Strip, the way was barred unless you got buzzed. So I tried to fit into the majority. I was drafted, tapped, frosted, and iced. Longnecks lured me to pitchers of pales and glasses of dark.

One night in a bar I don't remember with a mug of something I can't recall, I realized I had a problem. I don't like the taste of beer. I don't like it after two. I don't like it when it's new. I don't like it in a can. I don't like it. Do you understand?

So I tried to let it down easy. I nursed it awhile, spilled some accidentally. I forgot which mug was mine, forgot to get another.

But no one was fooled. When the last call sounded, I inevitably had sets of keys to cars I couldn't see out of or get out of but somehow drove anyway, trying to follow the garbled directions of mostly horizontal passengers. I guided the afflicted up staircases, into apartments, onto beds and left the trashcans by their heads. Being the designated driver sounds so heroic when Jimmy Smits plugs it on a TV spot. I wonder how many times he's had to hose off his car, his shoes, himself?

Waking up to find coffee ready to serve turned my life around. It's been a whirlwind romance. She's set up house for me in every part of town: the Old City, the Strip, in shopping centers, in bookstores. There she is brewing fresh and hot just for me. I don't have to hide my feelings anymore. There are places for my kind. I'm chic and trendy. I could be on TV.

I've gotten so hooked that I brought java home. She has space in the freezer and the kinds of mugs she's most comfortable in. I even have her picture framed in the wall clock I bought at Target. And my friends love what she can do to a Moravian cookie.

So when I socialize these days, I don't belly up to the bars. I approach the counters. I choose from lattes and au laits, from kaskas, from mochas. My shots are espresso. My refills are frothed on purpose. My cup runneth over with steam.

And when I get back to my table, I still remember who I'm talking to. In fact, we have long conversations fraught with meaning. We can even drive ourselves home afterwards. That's just one of the perks of seeking the short, dark, and roasted.

Next time you wake up heading for the mountains without going anywhere, ask yourself this. Was that really good to the last drop? You're only a cup away from a whole new lifestyle.

# Can You Hear Me Now?

"What brings you in?" the nurse wanted to know.

"This," I said, turning to show her the right side of my head.

"Oh, my God," she said.

And I felt so relieved. I wasn't the only one freaking out because I had a very large, red ear.

But it didn't stop there. The right side of my face was big and red as well. Plus, the red zone felt like putting my hand to a freshly boiled lobster.

This bizarre affliction developed overnight. I woke up only to land right back on my bed with a case of the spins as carousel-like as the time I drank too much wine at Allison's grandmother's wake and learned how walls can spin whether you look at them or not.

My co-worker, Kim, sat in the lounge of the walk-in clinic waiting to hear why I'd become a combination of red face/paleface.

Luckily, the doctor had a perfectly clear explanation. "I think it's an infection with a four-syllable medical name you've never heard before, much less had. Somehow it's affecting your ear and your skin at the very same time, although we have no idea why this is happening. But what I can tell you for certain is that no matter how bad you may feel right now, you definitely look even worse."

After shooting me full of an antibiotic I can't recall by name and adding a prescription guaranteed to make the yeast in me rise, the doctor ordered me back in twenty-four hours.

"How long will it take this to go away?" I asked, indicating the red face side of me.

The answer may have been anywhere from three to five days, but I understood what the doctor was really saying. It took mere hours to develop and would take the span of my adult life for full recovery.

Why me, I wondered, as people ogled me in my office like a sideshow attraction. From the left, she appears to be perfectly normal but when she turns, ladies and gentlemen, she becomes the nightmare you'll wake from screaming.

And as if to add to my despair, no one was taking the doctor's diagnosis at face value. "Maybe you have Ebola," my boss suggested.

"Botulism," another producer offered.

"Cat scratch disease," my vet student girlfriend decided, although she was calling from another state and had only my fever-enhanced description to go on.

But I knew what I had, a disease that only an artist could catch. I was suffering from Cubism, as sure as anyone Picasso ever painted.

Of course, Picasso wasn't really painting people who had bizarrely colored skin and freakishly large appendages on their heads— at least, not according to the art history books. They say he was making a point, or several points, depending on which painting you look at, to make geometry visible on a bunch of naked girls.

But my geometry teacher said that points, lines, and planes were a bunch of made-up theories just so we could do math. And I've always been mathematically challenged. So I think that before Picasso decided to revolutionize the art world, he must've seen a woman with a big, red ear and by bending it a little, he soon had her into his studio and onto his canvas. People not only want to stare at that, they pay good money for it and call it art.

Despite all the attention that having a swelled head brings, however, I was beginning to feel less like a revolutionary and more like I was being framed. That's when I tried to hide the truth about my condition with a sweater hood I found in my closet. Maybe I'd have gotten away with it too if it hadn't been the middle of July but, with the mercury hitting 90-plus day after day, nothing in my closet could keep my Cubism under wraps.

And then, what to my wondering eyes did appear, but there in the mirror, a flesh-colored ear. After seven days of drugs, one night of Reiki and a whole bottle of lotion for extra-dry skin, I had to face facts. My days of turning people's perceptions on their ears were over. I was healed. I was whole.

Yet I felt so empty, strangely emptier than I ever had before. Drivers didn't rubberneck when they went past. They didn't even hit the curb. Diners at the buffet didn't bump their heads on the safety shield anymore as the food they scooped fell short of their plates. And I didn't see anyone else in church keeping their eyes open while they prayed.

Oh, God. Just when I accepted that I'd be forced to lead a normal life, I realized it would only lead to unhappiness. I didn't want to fit into most people's perceptions. I wanted to stick out of them like a big, red ear. Can you hear me now? Cubism is my true calling.

I know this makes me part of a minority. Most studies estimate that only one out of every ten people is a Cubist. (I suspect that in Knoxville it's more like 1.5, but I'm not going to attempt a formal proof because I don't remember how.)

Of course, there are places where Cubists tend to concentrate. If you go to a play, you'll probably see Cubists. When you hire a decorator, he's probably a Cubist. When you hire a golf instructor, she's probably a Cubist. Look for people who challenge your perceptions. The man who's at his best in a dress and heels becomes every bit as obvious as a woman with a big, red ear.

So the next time you find yourself clutching a Crayola, color outside the lines, I dare you. And whether you auction the result at Sotheby's or eBay, remember, I deserve the credit. I'm the one with the swelled head.

# Costly Ways of Saving Money

Dear readers, I have discovered an incredibly innovative way to save money, if you're not me. You can join the library. There you can borrow all sorts of items to read or view or listen to, and when you're done you simply return them. Or until you're done, you can even renew them. But in my case, joining the library was a very costly decision. In fact, weeks later, I'm still paying it off.

I know what you're thinking. I went about this wrong. Well, I admit it. You're right. Are you satisfied now? But I got off to a perfectly good start, I assure you. I chose two unabridged novels on CD, *Hearts in Atlantis* and *White Oleander*. But I didn't read the free parking notice on the Lawson McGhee Web site before I went so I paid $2.00 to park downtown for thirty minutes. The good news is my library card was free.

*Hearts in Atlantis* is so long there are twenty CDs in the unabridged version. However, I've been known to re-read novels over nine hundred pages, so twenty CDs didn't seem like too much, before I started listening to them.

I listened for over four hundred miles, all the way to Macon, Georgia. I listened as I drove around Macon shopping, on breaks from a two-day college speaking engagement. I listened all the way back to Knoxville. I even listened while I ran errands on the weekend. That's when I noticed I was only on CD number 10 and the story, in my professional opinion, had mostly quit moving, much like driving on Broadway between traffic lights. Every glimmer of hope was simply a tease that disappeared as quickly as I stepped on the gas.

Woe is me, I thought, deciding it was time for a change of pace. So I put in some music and put CD number 10 somewhere in the car.

It may still be somewhere in the car, hiding, mocking me, knowing it's AWOL. But if it is, it's not under the floor mats. It's not in the back with the tire jack. It's not in the glove compartment, and it's not in the pocket I put on the sun visor. It's not even in the caddy where I keep the CDs.

As the due date approached, I decided to renew the set online to buy time until the missing item turned up. (Notice I didn't say until I found it.) It required only a matter of mouse clicks for me to renew *White Oleander*, along with the second set of *Hearts in Atlantis* CDs. My first set of *Hearts* was spoken for, however. In the time since I had checked it out, some evil person intent on exposing me had placed a hold on CDs 1-10 and the calendar said they were due the very next day.

So that night I paid a visit to Borders where I purchased the entire twenty CD set because that's the only way it was available. But I didn't mind paying $58 because the evil person who placed the CDs on hold would now have no reason to rat me out.

Unless, of course, the library cared what the CD looked like. Or unless I was trying to fool the librarian, who seemed to have a habit of flipping through the sets to make sure that all the CDs were, in fact, inside. The library version had a face that was plain, except for some writing that identified it. But from the gleaming surface of my newly purchased version, the face of Anthony Hopkins was staring at me. It could be because he starred in the movie, but I think it's really because he knew what I did. His character in the novel would've known in a heartbeat.

That's when I took some free advice from my co-worker Larry. Burn the CD, he said, and give the library that copy, then take your new copy back to Borders. They'll credit your card, and who's going to care? Well, except the library might get pissed off at you. They might call you in the middle of the night and play part of the CD where Anthony Hopkins sounds like Hannibal Lecter. "You know something happened, don't you? I think you do."

As I burned the CD, I turned the volume to mute. I also returned the set in the library's drop box where there were no prying eyes to inspect the contents. Then I walked in to have my parking ticket validated.

"There's no free parking in this garage," the librarian told me, pushing my ticket back across the counter. "You parked in the wrong one. The garage on Walnut Street is the one that's free." Thankfully, I found some change in the car. It cost 75 cents for five minutes inside.

And when I returned to Borders, I hardly fared better. "We can't credit your card," the woman told me, after I handed her the set of CDs. "We just give in-store credit when the shrink wrap is missing. See, it says so on the sign."

"You mean that big sign, right behind you?" I asked. "The one I didn't read when I bought the set?" I left my *Hearts* behind the cash register, in exchange for $58 in credit, good only at Borders for a limited time.

And so, dear readers, here's a final tally of the money I spent by joining the library. Parking downtown twice $2.75, set of twenty CDs at Borders $58, one gallon of gas, at least $1.38. But the joy I brought to some evil person who wanted my CDs at the cost of my admitting to illegal acts in print, well, that joy can't be tallied. It's truly priceless.

# Daytime Friends and Nighttime Lovers

"I used to be good to stay out till 2:00 or 3:00," my roommate said as she covered a yawn on a recent night out. "Now I can barely make it past 11:00. Are you about ready to go?" It was 10:45.

Another one bites the dust. I am losing friends. Not for any reason like they're moving away or find me insufferable. I'm losing friends because they're caving in to the urge to become daytimers.

Here's how the transition occurs, in case you're concerned about gradual changes in your own friends (or even yourself). First, they get a job where they work hours like 9:00 to 5:00. Shifts like this are called daytime hours. Then they start going home and having dinner. I believe these are often real dinners that come from cookbooks and require preparation. The next thing I know they're watching primetime TV when it's really on. They try to tell me about it, including the commercials, before I've had a chance to watch it on tape. Finally they're going to bed by 11:00, if not before. This is considered leading a "normal" life.

I wasn't told that there are alternative ways to live when I was growing up. It was assumed I would be "normal." I was a member of my minority for years without even realizing it. When I look back on my early life now, I realize I was just sleepwalking. I was giving in to family and peer pressure, desperate to seem part of the daytimer crowd, no matter what the cost. And when I moved out on my own, I was ashamed to be identified as someone who prefers the dark.

I remember it well, the night I realized I was different. Oh, I'll just come right out and say it, nocturnal. I am nocturnal. There, I'm out of the bed about it. I had friends over to watch a movie. It ended about 11:15 and I turned on the lights, ready for more pizza and in-depth discussions. What I got instead was a well-illuminated mass exodus from my apartment. "Thanks so much for the food. It was really good. And it's so great seeing you again but . . . we really have to go. Gotta be at work in the morning." Morning? They could work then with other people and be civil? It seemed so. In fifteen minutes, I was all alone and wide awake, no dream of mine.

Lately I've been thinking that my preference may be genetic. That seems like such a solid explanation. I was born this way. It's encoded in my genes, XXN. I can say to the daytimers I know, "How can you expect me to go against the makeup of my own DNA?" I even have evidence to support the genetic argument. I called my family's vacation condo at 10:45 one night. Out of six people, my mother was the only one awake. If she can pass male pattern baldness on to my brother, I don't see why she can't pass on nocturnal preferences to me.

So the reason I'm sitting up late drafting this soul-baring confession is that I hope to reach out to any of you who're feeling pressured to conform. You are not alone. It's okay if you're a nocturnal feeling forced to live a daytimer masquerade. Many of us have been there. Many of us have done that. Just face the fact that you may be subverting your true feelings, even from yourself. Don't discount the possibility too quickly. Think back with me. Remember . . . reading books by flashlight after you were supposed to be asleep? How the best pranks at camp were always pulled after dark? What a big deal it was to go to a midnight movie, breakfast after the prom, all-nighters in your dorm room? Take a deep breath and ask yourself some very important questions. Was I truly happy then? Have I ever been as happy since I left the night behind? If I could make the choice right now to live as a nocturnal, do I know that despite the hardships I would feel overwhelming joy at claiming my true identity?

If you answered yes to these questions, then your first step toward nocturnalness is easy to take. We have a wonderful piece of technology in our modern world that makes a night life more clearly possible than it ever was before. It's called the light bulb. Perhaps you're already familiar with it. It permits us to see after the sun goes down. It was invented by Thomas Edison who was fed up with people waking him at the crack of dawn. Rather than bow to the pressure of those persistent daytimers, Edison changed the world to suit his needs. And because he was willing to act on his true inclination, we have the power to overthrow the tyranny of the daylight hours, shine a beam of light into the darkness and proclaim ourselves free to stay up.

So the next time you feel yourself nodding off at 9:00 p.m., reach over and turn that switch. You'll be on your way to living the life you've only dared to dream about. "I love the night life. I got to boogie. On the disco ah hiiii, oh yeah."

# Pay Back

Recently I made a financial mistake. No, I didn't forget to pay a bill. I didn't bounce a check or forget to write one down. It was simpler than that, really. I looked to see what I owe.

I know, I know. What was I thinking? If you look before you write the check, you'll know for more than one day that you don't have enough money.

Anyway, there was the new amount staring me in the face. The amount that the great loan goddess SallieMae had determined I could now afford. (For those of you who haven't taken out school loans, SallieMae is the corporation that owns something like all of them. SallieMae, a name just like mom because you owe her big.) The amount I said could increase after two years because I'd surely be making more money after two years. Surely, I would.

I am making more money. In fact, I make thirteen dollars more per paycheck. That's a very tiny number, really. I stared at the new amount some more. The numbers there were very tiny too. If you want to get literal, they read fifty-eight dollars more per month is due starting now.

But I read those numbers as fifty-eight gazillion. I read them as: give us the children you don't have and your organs, major and minor. You don't need two eyes. You're not really using your pinkies either, except to type.

Many of you know what I had to do. Swallow my pride, steel my courage, call SallieMae and beg.

The following is an excerpt of the conversation I had with the loan counselor as it translated in my head.

COUNSELOR: For the past two years, you've been paying us one-quarter of your total income. That amounts to zilch.

ME: Zilch? But it's over five thousand dollars.

COUNSELOR: Those payments were only on your loan interest.

ME: Whose idea was that?

COUNSELOR: Yours, that's what you requested.

ME: Well, can't I just go on paying zilch? It feels like one-quarter of my total income to me.

COUNSELOR: Unfortunately, no. You'll have to recalculate your payments. You'll do that based on your income. I'll send you the paperwork.

ME: Calculate? I majored in liberal arts. Can you give me an idea what the payments will be with an estimate or something?

COUNSELOR: Sure. What do you make a month?

ME: Zilch.

COUNSELOR: Well, let's see 20 percent of that would be 220 gazillion dollars and you were paying 210 gazillion dollars already. So that shouldn't be a problem, right?

ME: Listen, I've got a nice appendix here and I'm not using it.

COUNSELOR: I'll get that paperwork right out to you. Thanks for calling.

ME: You're welcome. I'm so glad I went to graduate school.

COUNSELOR: We're glad we could help you.

When the paperwork arrived, I stared at the envelope for a while. I imagined that the calculations read something like this. If you take every dollar you make for the rest of your life and divide it by the amount that your loan increases due to interest each year, what will you have? Zilch. But you'll still owe us 30 gazillion dollars.

My fear was that the amount would calculate to more. I didn't know quite how that would happen, but I could imagine it all the same. I'd have to reduce my income. How to do that? Quit work. Oh, wait. Then I wouldn't have any income to make my payments. Oh, well. I broke open the envelope and dug out my calculator.

Seeing numbers like .00069 didn't help, but I finally got a result hours later when I was significantly balder. (Hey, maybe I could sell my hair and then . . . wait. That's another story.) The amount I owed came out to exactly one dollar less than I'm currently paying. Oh, the beauty of numbers. I really do make zilch. I can really only pay zilch. In fact, I've been overpaying.

I think I'm going to celebrate. Maybe I'll take myself somewhere nice and treat myself to dinner and a movie. But I have to make the credit card payment this week. Maybe I'll do it next week. No, I have to pay the cable bill, and then save so I can make the loan payment. Maybe I can do it the next week. No, then I have to make the loan payment. Hey, I'll have a dollar extra. I can see a movie months after its original release in a scary neon theatre with a bunch of kids who haven't even started earning zilch. But by God, I'll be there. I can't afford videos.

# Spacing Out

"I've been meaning to ask you," my roommate, Shannon, began, "don't you think it would work better if the TV was where the stereo is and the stereo was where the TV is?"

"I'll have to think about it," I said. What if she was right? What if they were easier to use if they were moved? What if this was true for other pieces of our furniture? What if we weren't making the best use of our space?

I have friends for whom space really is the final frontier. They boldly go where no one has gone before. At warp speed, they give rooms entirely new layouts. When I go to Jenny's or to Keytha's, I don't want to leave my chair even to go to the bathroom. What if it's not even in the same room anymore? Trust me, it's a distinct possibility.

The problem for me isn't that they rearrange with ease. It's that I've never been able to do it myself. My brain has never had that "look at a space and see it rearranged while everything sits still" function. The idea makes my eyes cross. I've always been a furniture setter-upper. I put all the furniture in a place when I move in, and then X years later when I move out, I move it.

But the other night when I put the TV where the stereo was, I could tell Shannon was right. It worked much better there. You could watch sitting on the couch *or* the futon. (Before you could only watch from the couch.) I turned to survey the space that surrounded me. I saw possibilities of rearrangement I'd never dreamt of before and it was only midnight.

When Shannon got up at 7:00 a.m. and walked through the living room, she found the TV and the stereo reversed, the speakers hooked up to play into both sides of the house, an end table by the TV, and an end table by the futon. She also found me, headed toward the dining room.

"Did you do all this last night?"

"I'm not done. I took the trunk out of the dining room and put it in my room. Now I'm going to move my desk and put my chair in the corner, and then we'll have room for a floor lamp. I'm going to price them at Target."

"See you later," she said, and peeled out of our driveway. I'm not sure what frightened her more— finding me up and speaking coherently at that hour, or wondering if any of the furniture would still be where it was when she got off work.

At Target, I saw multitudes of possibilities. There were floor lamps in a variety of styles and colors to suit the needs of the easy-chair reader. Corner-shelving units were made to neatly stack and display items in those hard-to-reach places in the house. There were even Mission-style chairs for the kitchen table, because wouldn't you rather be sitting on wood? Would they fit, I wondered? What did the legs measure?

Oh my God, I changed overnight. I'm not thinking like a furniture setter-upper anymore. In fact, I'm not even thinking like a furniture rearranger, not anymore. I've gone right into the next level. I'm thinking like a homeowner.

The next thing I know, I'll be going to Home Depot once a week. I'll pretend I need some potting soil, but I'll find my feet headed toward the home displays. I'll admire the countertops with the no-scratch finish. I'll wile away the hours selecting samples of floor coverings, considering kinds of wallpaper, deciding on just the right pair of drapes. I'll bring sample books home and ask my friends over for opinions. We'll discuss how a dishwasher really would round out the kitchen.

Wait a minute, wait a minute. Hello? Do I remember buying a house? Let's see…no. I remember signing a lease. Shannon and I signed a year's lease to rent a home. Not own it.

I edged away from the Mission chairs and took myself back to the floor lamp aisle. Box after box of lamps beckoned to me. Wouldn't it be nice to see and read? Yes, it would, but that was beside the point because I can't afford one right now. The rent is due this week.

As I arrived back at home, the phone rang. It was my landlady. She wanted to know if tomorrow would be a good day to deliver our new dishwasher with a no-scratch, butcher-block countertop on it. The dishwasher would be billed to her and her husband, the homeowners, who can afford it, even this week.

Now you tell me, what's the harm in thinking like a homeowner if I get to have my cake and eat it off a plate cleaned in a brand new dishwasher too?

# Give Till It Hurts

What's your name? (What's your name?) Who's your daddy?
(Who's your daddy?) Is he rich? (Is he rich like me?) Has he
taken any time? (Any time?) to show, to show you what it
means to shop? Tell it to me slowly. Tell you why, I really want
to know. It's the time of the season for shopping.

Right now most Americans are at the mall, the mart, the
market, the maxx. Like salmon, they're spawning toward the
neon sale signs and flashing blue lights. Now ask yourself
something, if you're one of the multitudes fighting for a parking
place, fighting to get in the door first, settling for a sweater two
sizes too small because you're determined to put something in
a box for your brother. Are you having any fun? If everyone
else was swimming upstream to spawn and die, would you?

I've been there, tried that, and it's not my kettle of fish.

Knowing I'm not a shopper myself, some of my friends
tried me on as a consultant. Will Fill-in-the-Blank Relative like
whatever object I'm currently showing you? Does the dress/un-
derwear/pair of socks go with all the other things I'm buying?
Is the serving tray/crock-pot/water filtering pitcher going to
hold enough? Would a riding mower be the better way to go,
to mow? They want to know.

After a great deal of market research, careful consideration
of product strengths versus weaknesses, and a lot of waking up
in displays I don't recall seeing before, I've developed a stan-

dard response. I have no idea. It used to be I don't care, but somehow I always ended up holding the bags and the car was parked farther away.

Home, home for a change. That place I've dreamed of all day.

Yes, another Hanukkah and Kwanzaa and Christmas are almost upon us. This time a realization has occurred to me. There are shoppers and there are what I am, a minority. But I'm a minority crying out to finally be recognized, in *Time* magazine, on *Primetime,* and even on *Oprah.* Our families don't have to hide us anymore. We are the getters. Got it? Good.

Here's how to recognize us. When you see us in stores, we're looking for some specific thing or things we need or for some reason want very much. When we catch the scent, we respond lightning quick. We grab, hang on, and we don't share. We've even been known to swallow things whole.

We drift along in the current with ease. But we never go out looking for nothing because we're sure we'll come home with it. Then what will we have to show for ourselves?

The most important thing you can remember about getters is this. When we find what we're looking for, we're ready to go home. If you insist on dragging us around with you, you'll probably hear one of the following complaints. 1) My feet hurt and I already have what I need. 2) The benches make my butt numb and I already have what I need. 3) I don't want to stay here while you try on everything in the store. 4) And did I mention I already have what I need.

Shoppers, here's my advice to you. Don't be insulted or frightened by the getters in your life. We didn't ask to be different. We just got recessive genes. Everybody used to go out looking for something. Some of us lost interest once the prey quit moving and the entire village wasn't dependent on us for the next meal anymore. The thrill is gone. The thrill is gone away.

For those of you who mutated into commercially driven, subliminally influenced homo sapiens using as many charge cards as there are letters in your name, I wish you a joyous holiday season. May you look long hours for everything on your many lists. May you need something from every store in town. May you get down to that one item you just can't locate. But may you find that perfect gift at the very last minute in the very last place you ever would've looked. May you need it wrapped. May you wait in line for two hours the very next day to exchange it because your mother/sister/aunt bought them the very same thing and you can't find the receipt even though you know you kept it somewhere.

As for myself, and the other getters I know, we're celebrating the season in our own way. We searched the Internet and we already have what we need.

# Speed Freak

"Do you want to drive?"

No was all I had to say, one simple word. But no.

Jenny had been driving my car back from Nashville. We'd dropped Brock off. We were five minutes from our respective homes. Everything was going smoothly.

So of course I took the wheel. A car in front of us had a bumper sticker that read "Just say no." I passed it.

Halfway down Lonas, a cop stepped into the road. He pointed at us. Then he pointed to a street that turned right.

I slowed, turned, and looked for the accident he was directing us around. I wondered about all the other cars pulled over. "Aren't you going to stop?" Jenny finally asked.

"Stop for what?"

"Stop so he can write you a ticket."

I'd been nailed after all this time. The truth about me was going to become a matter of public record. Hi, my name is Angie. I'm a speeder. I'll probably speed again.

Truth be told, I've been speeding for years and I'm not alone. At least 10 percent of the population speeds. Or it could be even more. That's what I've heard. Studies are being done. Is it in the genes? Is it taught in childhood? Does exposure to other speeders raise the odds? Do we speed to rebel against authority? Do speeders have some kind of natural radar? As a speeder, I have to tell you, I couldn't drive any other way. It just feels right.

When the officer handed me my citation, he said, "This date is when you have to appear in court, Ma'am."

Court? Excuse me? Court is for criminals or people getting divorced, not me, not a speeder. I couldn't plead out of something I do by instinct. It's unnatural. There is a cog in my wheel.

I called the next day to investigate my non-court options. I had one, pay the fine. How much, I asked while eyeing my checkbook, more inclined at the time to bounce than behave. It wasn't good news. Going forty-eight in a thirty zone is eighty-something dollars, plus change. "That's one-third of what I make in a week," I blurted. "Maybe you should slow down," the clerk suggested. I hung up instead. I had begun to question my driving style.

During the period it took me to raise the money, I attempted living my life as though I'm a driver. I stayed in the right-hand lane as much as possible, kept one eye on my speedometer at all times, forced my foot to ease off the gas, and told myself there was no reason to hurry to work. I even caught myself rejoicing when a cop pulled over the guy who was passing me, that is, after I quit hyperventilating and pulled back onto the road.

But the day I mailed the check with my citation, I noticed my car creeping back over the centerline into the left lane. As I leaned closer to the wheel and got a better grip, I focused both eyes on the road ahead, where they remained, except to check the price of gas, of course. And when the man with the thinning hair veered in front of me in his pick-up, I accelerated past him in such a burst that my car truly earned the name on its front license plate, Sputnik.

I feel I owe it to my parents to admit that I wasn't raised this way. My father always knows the speed limit on every road we're on. He frequently asks if I know it while looking at my speedometer, then looking at me. What puzzles him is how I can willfully do something that will cost me one-third of what I make in a week, if caught.

I have only one answer. It's simple, really. I cannot deny my true identity. I tried. But I feel like the Bionic Woman trying to convince you I'm hurrying while really going in slow motion with cheesy sound effects.

I'm a speeder born with a lead foot. (Maybe it comes from my mother's side.) I was raised in a series of Ford sedans when V8s were family cars and backseats were roomy. I'm a firm believer that riding the brakes is a sin and other drivers must be gotten around before they get in my way, if at all possible.

So, get out of my way. I'm a girl on the go. Speedy Acres is the place to be. Fast driving is the life for me. See ya.

# Thirty Something

I did something not long ago that startled people. I turned thirty willingly, admittedly even. So sue me for going against the majority rule, okay? The one where you're supposed to tell people you're twenty-nine for several years, then start admitting you're over thirty by making jokes about it. "I'm only over thirty now that no one in dark restaurants will card me." I saw a limb and went right out to the very end of it. I even bounced around, proudly declaring, "I'm thirty" for anyone who wanted to listen, or didn't.

Then it happened. I dreamed I was in a Peanuts cartoon. Charlie Brown asked me why Lucy always pulls the ball away at the last minute. I opened my mouth to answer. "Wah wah, wah wah wah wah," I said.

Oh God, I'm one of them, an adult. Just call me ma'am.

Are you talking to me? Sorry, I can't hear you. I'm having an identity crisis. I know that adults are supposed to have planned their lives, improved their health, become enlightened, and prepared for retirement, all at the same time. But I'm not sure I'm ready for that. I just now got good at sharing my toys. Well, some of them, maybe. Did you ask nice?

Adults are like the Army, though. They're always looking for recruits. They'll go in undercover and their goal is to make you think like they do.

Here's the scary thing. I think they've gotten to me. I'm eating vegetables now. I'm talking platefuls of veggies, regularly. I have a counter full of facial products that I bought. I joined a gym. I work out three times a week. I use the word "buff" to describe myself. I'm even in a prayer support group. That means several people are trying to figure out what to do with my life.

And there's more. I want things I don't need just because other people have them. For instance, I want a real job. I don't mean the kind I do forever, just the kind where I make a lot of money so I can afford a four-wheel drive. Going up Seventeenth Street in the snow, through the floods on Kingston Pike, and down the gravel-strewn ruts of Middlebrook Pike is possible in an Escort, but it looks classier in a Land Rover. I want a cell phone too so that people who are stuck in traffic can call me because they can't drive over the median since they don't have four-wheel drives. And I want a vacation home where I can go when I'm tired of working at my real job, driving my four-wheel drive, and talking on my cell phone.

But I won't get any of these things because adults have to plan for the future. This involves creating things that will last after you're dead or after you retire, whichever comes first. So I bought into a mutual fund to go with my 401(K). I don't re-ally understand how they work. I just know that I can't buy a house, get married, or have children because I'm saving all of my money to throw myself a really nice funeral which I won't see even though I'm the guest of honor.

Here's my assessment of being an adult so far. Even though I'm eating things that are slimy, I still have to take more vitamins than I did when I ate fast foods. I need a lot of cosmetics now, but I've never worn makeup. I pay to get into a place where I do things that make my muscles hurt, yet I keep going and paying them. I want to buy the toys that all the other grown-ups are playing with, but I don't want to spend the next thirty-two years paying for them. So I'm saving up for the day when

I won't be around to enjoy all this. And because I've gotten in touch with my spiritual side, I can identify all of my hang-ups and share them with you, openly, honestly, and lovingly.

Now, you want my advice? Don't be all that you can be if it involves doing things before 9:00 a.m. Be young, be foolish, be happy. Be twenty-nine for as long as you can fool anybody, including yourself.

# Getting Your Jollies

Long, long ago in the 1970's in a galaxy far, far away called the Tri-Cities at a tiny grocery store by the name of Giant, I first saw the figure that towered over produce and still does. He's as green as spinach without any dressing. He's as long and solid as a freshly washed cucumber, as covered with leaves as a new head of lettuce. He's known far and wide as the Jolly Green Giant, the lord of the vegetables. Whether steamed, cooked or fried, he dishes them out to everyone but me.

Let me settle onto the couch and explain the root of the problem. (Get it, root?) When I was a child, I ate as a child, meaning nothing good for me. Naturally colorful, vitamin-enriched, sugarless foods had no appeal. They were stringy, slimy, and chewy, not to mention the way they smelled. So I'm not mentioning it.

But there was another reason. I couldn't explain it back then. Now that I'm thirty something, however, I can spill the beans with the greatest of ease.

Call me Monica. Give me a beret. I'm here to expose the sordid fact that the Giant wants to keep hidden from the public eye. It's an awful truth that could spread in scandal rags until his good name is compost, until everything he supposedly stands for is congealed like a set-in stain on the American public.

The Jolly Green Giant isn't jolly. He's lying to you, just like he lied to me. Though he runs campaigns featuring the word

"Jolly" as part of his name, throws his hands on his hips and "ho, ho, ho's" as loud as St. Nick, he isn't playing the field. He's tilling it.

In produce, where I used to see him on a regular basis, he wore nothing short of a lip-pursing, eyebrow-scrunching, jaw-squaring scowl pointed right at me. I knew what that meant then and I still do. Don't just eat your vegetables today. Eat them now. No excuses. Clean your plate. Do you want a good spanking?

He knows when I eat healthy. He knows when I do not. And he's got much more than a lump of coal in store for me. Without what he provides, my face will shrivel, then the rest of me. I'll never be one with my bathroom unless I drink powders that remain the consistency of sand, despite constant stirring. And I'll only see 20/20 in my mind's eye before long.

It's not that being healthy feels bad. It's just that I've never been willing to cower my way into a better lifestyle letting a big liar get the last "ho." So I spent my formative years as the poster child for Oscar Mayer and Velveeta. Now look at me. I'm five feet of sculpted muscle wrapped around a killer immune system, topped off with (still) naturally non-gray hair. Processed meat and cheese foods, they did a body good.

That is, until about a year ago when my taste was spoiled permanently by a dish of a woman, a true blue plate special, my friend Sara. She's also known as Madam Vegetable. She's all of the things the Giant is not - honest, real, nice, reasonably sized, female, steamy, dicey, a good dresser, and has real hair. (She's more inclined to wear green linen than green leaves.) The greater the pressure, the more she cooks. And when she throws her hands on her hips and laughs, the sound comes from her diaphragm.

I remember the first time she fed me dinner. We didn't discuss the menu. It was an impromptu thing. I sat down. She served broccoli to the left of me, corn to the right, and cabbage in the far corner. Cauliflower came next, then peppers. She didn't know about my Giant problems or my new dilemma. How could I explain I was opposed to every plateful of food before me? I sized her up. All she was saying, it seemed, was give vegetables a chance.

So I did. The corn I bit into was good so I crunched some cauliflower which was even better and that led me to cabbage which couldn't get any better but I still wanted more as I speared the broccoli and oh my God it was so good that when I got to the peppers I just couldn't take it anymore, more, more...It was beyond my wildest dreams. Oh my God. It was all so good, so good, so very, very good. The Giant would never have done this for me.

But Madam Vegetable isn't satisfied yet. My habits displease her. My diet is lacking. Bologna makes her cringe, along with canned ravioli. Even Pop-Tarts are what she calls a last resort. (They have eight vitamins and minerals, though. It says so on the box. Frosting added to that doesn't seem like a big deal, does it? But I digress.)

This is what it boils down to. I've been cleansing my palette just to please her. That's how it started out anyway. Now, I'm doing it because I like it. I want more. I can't get enough or make do with a frozen entrée on the side anymore.

I don't need professional help. I already have it. We're consenting adults, the Madam and I. So I can admit this in public without fear of repercussions from my supposed peers. Without fear that one day, I'll run across a dress I just happened to keep. She'll say, "Do I see some sort of stain on there?" I'll say, "It certainly isn't from a pepperoni log that I had for dinner one night, only one night, a long time ago. I haven't hurt anyone, much." We'll never have a scene like that in front of everyone. What would be the point?

# *Play It Again?*

A NOTE BEFORE READING: If this starts to sound familiar to you, here's a little something you should probably do. Read it to the rhyme of the Grinch and the Whos.

On a night back in April, not too long ago, my friend Annalee and I went to a show. At the Tennessee Theatre where seats were arrayed, Ani DiFranco sang music and played.

Now Ani is angry in some of her songs. Her guitar and her drums and her lyrics are strong— which is probably why grunge kids of all shapes and sizes can't get enough of her songful surmises.

And there on that night something happened to me that was odd in the least. I am sure you'll agree.

Every grunge kid on the floor liked the concert a lot. But I, seated up in the balcony, did NOT!

It *could* be my hair wasn't corn rowed just right. It *could* be that my Aigner dress shoes were too tight. But I think that the most likely reason of all was PMS making my pants feel too small.

Whatever the reason, my PMS or my shoes, I sat in that balcony hating the youths. All that night long, I could find nothing pleasing. I hated the grunge and I hated the sleazing.

I enjoyed Ani's music of two years before, but something had changed. I could hear her no more. Did she sing about girls? Did she sing about boys? All I heard was the Noise! Oh, the NOISE! NOISE! NOISE! NOISE!

THEN the grunge kids did something I liked least of all. Every grunger in Knoxville, the tall and the small, all stood close together with amps and drums ringing. They stood hand-in-hand and they all started singing. They sang! *And they sang!* AND they SANG! SANG! SANG! SANG! till my ears RANG and RANG! How they RANG! RANG! RANG! RANG!

Then those grungers, they danced. Oh, those grungers, they swayed. How the hips of those grungers got in my way. It was worthless to pay for the seat I sat in when all of their seats would constantly get in my small field of view. I really was frettin.'

It was about this time that I took a good look at the clothes I was wearing. I was in the wrong nook with my pants of stretch nylon and my shirt of long sleeves. I didn't fit in with the cut-offs and tees. (Not to mention my nylon wasn't stretching enough. Even though I looked nice, I was having it rough.)

So I decided to imagine some things in my head that would cause me to enjoy myself more instead.

While the grunge kids were passed out at home in their beds, I'd sneak in their rooms and put hair on shaved heads. I'd trim ratty braids without charging a fee. I'd recolor dye jobs more eye pleasingly. Why, the grunge kids would all look salon-styled like me.

As a clothing crusader, I would do what I could to redress these grunge kids and make them look good. I'd put shirts on bare chests, no more tank tops a-slidin, and pants on the butts with no underwear hidin.'

I'd toss worn-out Doc Martens all splattered with booze, Birks with cork soles that were starting to ooze, and All-Stars too grimy for Goodwill to use. I'd educate these grungers on shoe wear and care, even staying until I'd reviewed every pair.

Back in the theatre, I'd clear the whole balcony, no dancing, no standing, and no smooching in front of me. I'd sit in the comfort of my nice, padded chair and I'd watch unobstructed. It seems only fair.

I'd tape mouths of the yellers and singers. It's true. "I'm glad you love Ani. I'm sure she is too, but I came to hear her, not any of you." Then she'd step to the mic to sing meaningful songs. And I'd know all the words, not sing loudly along.

I'd take beer and IDs from all grunge underagers, leaving ten of us legal, including onstagers.

To finish things off with a final grand coup, I'd round up their lighters and cigarettes too. Then those grunge kids in Knoxville would all cry BOO-HOO!

With that, I came back to the kids and the noise. I looked all around me at the grunge girls and boys. And I had to admit that on days way back when, I actually resembled a fair lot of them.

But now I've turned into an old concert prude, as was recently suggested by my good friend Jude. Take a walk in my Aigners before you decide that I'm pre-menopausal and postal besides. And to grungers in Nashville for the third Lilith Fair, I hope that you're ready 'cause I'll see you there.

# Close Encounters of My Own Kind

The story you're about to hear is strange but true. The other night, I sat down on my couch. Then I decided to lie down. I was tired. It could happen to anyone. An hour later when I woke up, I noticed something. It was only 11:00. This never happens to me. Something's wrong and I know what it is. After numerous years as a nocturne, it's finally happened. I've been abducted, reprogrammed, and turned into a daytimer. Yikes. If it can happen to me, you could be next. But remember, my friends, the truth is out there.

I've been trying to pinpoint how I was selected. Being an easy mark had something to do with it, I'm sure. There I was roaming on the outskirts of the herd already, flaunting my nocturnal status for all to see. Being offered a new job should've tipped me off. "Work as a full-time writer," they said, "In your own office at your own desk, nine to six on weekdays. Doesn't that sound good? For double your present pay?"

"The price is right. When do I start?" was all I had to say to activate the tiny chip in my neck that signals the mother ship to come on down.

Here's how I know this isn't all in my head. On the Internet, I found a list of fifty-two indicators for UFO encounters or abduction by aliens. Right away, I recognized my own frequently occurring new experiences. (I'm covering the reasons out of sequence so you'll feel as confused as I do.) "Reason number sixteen: awakened in the middle of the night **startled**." Six-thirty is the middle of the night, as far as I'm concerned. Yet my alarm clock keeps going off at that hour. I can't even begin to tell you how startled I am by this.

Then there's "reason number fourteen: **awakened in another place** than where you went to sleep, or don't remember ever going to sleep." I don't recall getting in bed for the past several nights. I remember lying on the couch watching TV. Then my alarm clock is going off and its 6:30 again, but I'm in bed. How spooky is that?

Moving on to "reason number one: have had **missing or lost times** of any length, especially one hour or more." Not only does this fit in with the above reason, it also describes what happens to me from 6:30 to 8:00 in the morning, which is that I have no idea what happens to me. My roommate, Mary, may have said or asked me something over lunch, I mean breakfast. (See? I'm really losing time. I'm typing actual Freudian slips now, not pretending to type them.) "Wah wah, wah wah wah wah," is what I heard her say. I don't know what I told her. What if I'm supposed to get something from the store like tampons or chocolate? Maybe it was ice cream. Was it chocolate ice cream? Mary, phone home. No, wait, I'm not at home. Am I? Where am I?

In any case, this brings me to "reason number twenty-five: have been suddenly **compelled to drive or walk** to an out-of-the-way or unknown area." Suddenly work compels me to drive for at least thirty minutes to get there. Then people I've never seen before stop by my office to ask what I'm doing. "I don't know," I want to say. "Can you tell me? My appointment book says lunch at Luby's Cafeteria. Who am I meeting? And where's the Hot Bagel Company? Why do I feel compelled to go there for coffee when I don't even know what street it's on?"

I looked on a map, though. All the unknown locales are in Oak Ridge, a daytimer hangout for years. And a lot of what goes on there is top secret, government cover-up sorts of things. I've heard that from several sources who shall remain nameless.

"Reason number twenty-nine: have heard **strange humming or pulsing** sounds, and could not identify the source." This happens every time I nod off during the day. But I'm sure it's not the computer I work on. Why would I hear it humming just because I have my head on it?

"Reason number fifty: have the feeling that you are **not supposed to talk about these things,** or that you should not talk about them." I can write about them, though. I have the feeling that's okay.

"Reason number fifty-one: have tried to resolve these types of problems with **little or no success.**" This is so true. Of course, I'm working in my field for the first time in my life, making twice what I was a month ago. Could it be that my heart's not in to going back to my pre-abducted state? No, no, that's too obvious.

The thing is I'm really afraid I'm going to be abducted again. I've heard it usually happens more than once. This is how it will go, I suppose. Some night I'll nod off early on the couch to awake feeling different. I'll look around and lo and behold, I'll be in a bigger house that I've never seen before. In the driveway, there'll be a car I don't remember buying. It will be something fun and fast and four-by-four with my name on the key ring hanging by the door. There won't be any student loan bills in the mail on the table. Then I'll hear someone coming in, saying, "Honey, I'm home." I'll pinch myself. Ouch, better try that again. Ouch, look, I know this is a conspiracy. Ouch, you can't fool me. It's time for some total disclosure. At least I think so, maybe.

# A Girl by Any Other Name

When we swept into The Carousel, every eye was not on me, despite my tempting T-shirt, pant-for-me plaid shorts and succulent sneakers. The eyes, instead, were on the cascades of curls, the form-fitting, fawn-colored dress, and the rhinestone-studded pumps of the woman beside me, my friend Maria. And I want you all to know something. I was just fine with that.

It's time for me to come out of the closet. Many women toss on dresses and heels with the greatest of ease, but I'm not that kind of girl. My slips are hanging. Sorry, Mom. I know you tried to transform me, but let's give Dad his due. I entered this world as an XXY, a tomboy.

Early in my life the truth was apparent, but it was the early '70s when even men were dressing up like girls. I could see only one way to fit in, cognito, and disguise. I did church in dresses and tights, baked cakes, learned to sew, had my room painted pink, put up Leif Garrett pictures facing my bed.

But it didn't take long for my personalities to split. A picture of the Bionic Woman in the mail set off the schism. She didn't have her hair in a Wonder Woman bouffant or spin around till her red, white, and blue corset appeared. No, Jaime Somers, with her locks floating freely over her shoulders, was saving the world in jeans and a white shirt. I took Leif down and put Jaime up. It just felt right.

That was when I started wearing the pants in my family. I

even added an occasional ball cap. Soon I had my own football, my own bat, my own glove. My rod and my reel, they comforted me. On the days when my cakes fell, they comforted me.

And then, along came the decade when girls started dressing like boys, wholesale. That was the '80s. Overnight my quirks turned into chic, but living at home cramped my style. My mother still expected me to turn into the girl of her dreams, so I led her on the best way I knew how. I became a cross dresser. I'd leave for school as a girl in an initialed sweater, jeans, deck shoes, and an add-a-bead necklace for that extra touch.

But the moment I got to school...Shazam! I transformed into the true me. My dad's dress shirt draped below my knees; my thrift-store tie whipped from side to side; my borrowed blazer billowed; my jazz shoes shuffled to a synthesized beat. A single pearl earring finished off the effect.

The girl I left behind wadded into the bottom of my book bag until five minutes before Mom picked me up.

That worked just fine for four years until something else happened. It was something as inevitable as the resurgence of bell bottoms and disco. I grew up. (Some who know me would argue this point, but my bones have fused and I'm legal for everything.)

My advice is, don't try this at home. Being a grown-up boy is like wearing a shoe that doesn't fit. Look at Peter Pan, for instance. He flies around in a skirt, tights, and slippers and lives in a place called Never-Never Land. He also bears a strong resemblance to Sandy Duncan. Does this sound balanced to you? Just say no.

Here's my solution for you. Dare to be different, to truly stand out. In no time, you'll be in. Leave those formals on their hangers, ladies, those pumps on the racks, that hairspray in a can.

And be a real boy if he's the real you. Wear ball caps on good hair days as well as bad ones. Wear out the knees of your jeans and refuse to have them patched. Track in dirt without noticing. Climb every tree, the higher the better. Never admit to getting stuck. Stomp in every puddle. It's your sacred right to splash farther than anyone has ever splashed before. Make car noises even when you're not driving. Play with tools. Hammer in the morning. Hammer in the evening. Hammer all day long. You go, girl. Let's see some hustle out there.

# Just Shoot Me

"What's hurting?" the nurse asks me.

"My lower back."

"How does it hurt?"

"I'd like to die. Could you shoot me, please?"

"I'm afraid not."

"Coward."

Last week I bent down to pet the cat and I heard this odd sound. It came from my back. It sounded like I broke something. In fact, it felt like I broke something but, since all I did was bend down to pet the cat, I went back to writing at my computer. Hey, I'm no fool.

I don't know why it happened, but a couple of hours later I could swear an invisible person was stabbing me in the left kidney. Countless ibuprofen and videos later, I could tell no change except that it took me longer to come to that conclusion.

So I went to see my massage therapist, Sara. (You may remember her as Madam Vegetable.) She asked me where I hurt, then put her thumb exactly in the center of my pain and pressed.

"!@#$%^&*)(_+!"

"You've pulled one of your external rotator muscles. I'm going to stretch it for you."

"Can't you just shoot me?"

"I'm more humane than that," she said with a smile.

So by the next day, I had completely recovered. I took it easy, rested, took ibuprofen (well, one more at least) and went to New Orleans at the end of the week. Then I walked everywhere in the wrong shoes for three days in a row on concrete sidewalks, brick cemeteries, and the hardwood floors of our rooming house with Sara. My friend Shannon, a physical therapist who was also on the trip, told me I was crazy. (And as it happens, she was right.)

That brings me back to where I began this— in the doctor's office in a great deal of pain. "It hurts when I breathe," I finally tell the nurse who turns me over to the x-ray technician.

In the freezer where she works, she makes me lie down on a hard, sub-zero table. Then she arranges me like we're playing Twister only I'm in pain and she's calling the shots. She makes me hold my breath. She aims. She fires. (Alas, only with rays of radiation which kill too slowly for my taste.) Then she arranges me into another pretzel-style target. I'd like to say I lost all feeling, but I didn't. I felt so much by that point, I really had no words to express it.

Back in the room, the doctor finally arrives. "Does it hurt here?" he asks. Then he stabs me in the back just like the invisible person who started all this. If I wasn't in so much pain, I would shoot him— before shooting myself, that is.

When I can speak again, I tell him that it does hurt where he stabbed me. In fact, it hurts even more than it did before.

Finally he tells me that I'm in pain. I've hurt the muscle where he just stabbed me. Then he writes prescriptions for me to get drugs. (Will they interfere with my ability to aim at myself, I wonder?) And he sends me to physical therapy.

"Would you like us to stretch that sore back?" a therapist asks me.

Is this a trick question? I ask in my head.

"My ride's on the way," I say, and pray that at any moment Kellye will arrive and, although she's been refusing to shoot me all day, this time she'll change her mind. She'll see me in pain and take pity on me. She'll reach in her purse, whip out a revolver, and do away with me because that's what friends are for.

Instead, Kellye takes me to get the drugs. However, they don't have me in the filing system on their computer. The pharmacist asks me to come back in fifteen minutes.

"Can't you just shoot me?" I ask. "Then I won't need to come back at all. You could even have my prescriptions. They're supposed to make you feel much better."

"I can't do that," she says. "It's illegal to take someone else's prescriptions."

Where are your values these days, people? That's what I'd like to know. You'll drive by and shoot a perfect stranger standing on the corner. You'll shoot somebody you know when they're yelling at you. You'll shoot somebody who catches you doing something illegal. But you won't shoot your friend who's been asking politely all day. Were you raised in a barn? That is just so rude.

I'm going to put up a bunch of billboards around town. That's a great way to make a point. They'll say, "Is your neighbor in pain? Don't let her turn to painkillers. You love her enough to help her put an end to her suffering, don't you? Of course you do. So shoot her."

God, I feel better just thinking about it.

# I Am Not Your Handy Man

I've been operating under a mistaken identity until quite recently. I've been convinced that I am handy, but moving into a new house has done what nothing else could. It's outed me. I'm just wearing a tool belt so I can pass. Those who are really handy sense the truth. I have the equipment but not the know-how. (Not enough, anyway. Oh, the shame, the shame.)

When I couldn't connect the dryer by myself and yelled, "!&*$!" so loudly that my roommate and her boyfriend came to help, I began to question my calling. When the second set of bathroom shelves (first set was too tall AFTER assembly) just missed my head on their way to the floor, I grew confused. (Perhaps those shelves did clip me on the noggin after all.) When I drilled myself in my own !@&*%*! arm, I finally had to acknowledge the truth.

I'm lacking something and it's not common sense, despite what you may think. There is some sort of handy gene that's been stolen from my pool. There are handy traits that were never passed on to me. There's a handy kit I can never find for sale.

I see other women being handy. I'm not saying they're in the majority, mind you, but I'd guess that at least one out of every ten females is handy or has dabbled with being handy at some point in her life.

I know I'm one of these handy women. I feel a kinship with

them I can't explain. It's just an innate part of me. So I buckle my belt. I wield my screwdriver. And still, I can't get my closet door open. "Who took the !@#$%! doorknob off, anyway?"

This doesn't add up. I've watched the men in my family being handy for generations. My great-grandfather was handy. My grandfather was handy. My father is handy. I just want to be the family handy woman. Is that so wrong?

I got off to the right start. I can tell you that. I was born with a hammer in my hand. I hammered in the morning. I hammered in the evening. I hammered all day long. My father still has wood blocks with the gazillions of nails I drove into them. You wouldn't find me in a pair of high heels, playing with a tube of lipstick. When I was a child, I pulled on my overalls and hammered as a child.

Now that I'm grown, I have to disinfect my own drill wounds. But while I was disinfecting ("Ow! !@*^#%!, it!"), I realized something. I never did that many handy things myself. I mostly held things while my father was being handy. I held the screwdrivers, the wrenches, the flashlight, the measuring tape, even the occasional chalk line. (But I didn't walk it.)

He was the one doing the connecting, and the assembling, and the putting up of new items. I suppose I could've asked him questions like, "If it doesn't say on the box, how do you tell the size of something without assembling the item in question?" But I was so good at holding and hammering, I thought I could get by.

I just got off the phone with my father. He's working on my house while I'm not there. (Imagine my eyebrow raised because it is.) He and my mother have set up my bedroom furniture and, since I left the new doorknob lying by the door, the door I couldn't get open, that is, he's done it for me. Subtle, aren't I?

So I get brave. I ask him about the shelf brackets I put on my bathroom wall. "They're not level, are they?"

"Did your shelves fall down? You have to push the arms that hold them till they click in place. Did you hear them click?" !$#!, they click? "I might not have done that."

I have to face facts. I know what to do. Ignoring it won't work any longer. I have to let go of my anger !*@%#^$! it. I have to forgive my parents for not raising me to be the handy woman I know I am. (They did give me all the tools I could ever use, after all.) I have to put on my tool belt, look at myself in my mirror and say, "I'm handy enough, I'm woman enough and, doggone it, people like me."

I have to start hanging out with other handy women. There may be a handy support group I can join to get in touch with my own inner handiness. (But not too in touch. That's a bit of a touchy area.)

I have to shop at Home Depot, regularly. I have to stroll down the aisles, realizing that in a very real way, I've come home. I have to watch HGTV regularly, respecting Bob Villa's practicality and recognizing the underlying handiness of Martha Stewart. (Even if she's more inclined to cook my goose than clean my pipes.)

I have to start collecting books about being handy. I have to read them till the spines are cracked and loan them to others seeking advice and illustrations about being handy.

And most of all, when I see another woman, perhaps wearing a skirt and squinting through her glasses, struggling to get a screw into a hole, I have to be willing to lend her a hand. Or two.

# I Don't

Women. I should know better by now than to befriend them. Sooner or later, no matter how casual I try to keep things, they always start to get serious on me. I tell them I'm not the one they want. I'm a free spirit, I say. That kind of responsibility would weigh me down. But they don't care that I'm not ideal. Their sights are set on commitment; the clock is ticking; and when they pop the question, it really comes as no surprise. "Angie, will you be in my wedding?"

"Look, I like you and all. I really do. But I just don't know if I feel that way about you." That's what I should say the next time it happens. But I'm just a girl who can't say no.

This is why I told my friend, Dixie, I would do her the honor. Although, with my thirty-something years of brides-maid experience, I already knew what was going to happen. I'd suck at doing what was expected of me. She'd feel let down. I'd feel guilty. And she'd eventually decide we were better off as friends.

Of course, that never happens until after the ceremony. My freaking out, however, started with the fitting. To say that the taffeta two-piece enveloped me really doesn't do it the justice it deserves. To say that my periwinkle, non-petite skirt flowed so far onto the floor behind me that it created a train to rival the bride's, that would paint you a more colorful picture. To say that my sleeveless top sagged so far down my shoulders that it looked like a garter with the elastic nearly gone, that would truly be more accurate. And to say that I was surrounded by young brides-to-be whose estrogen levels were off the charts, that would give you a more distinctive description of the day I dropped in at David's Bridal "I need a Midol" Shop.

In the midst of my trauma, the employee who was helping me try to stay dressed appeared with a sandal that had a heel so high it literally sent me over the edge. Even though she offered me a free dye job, I turned her down flat, which you may have seen coming. But it made beating a path to the front counter so much easier.

Let me assure you, I'm not cut out to be your bridesmaid. When it leads me to question my identity to the point that I barely recognize my own reflection, I think it's time to leave you at the altar, but no hard feelings, okay? This is all about me.

When I arrived for alterations after my initial fitting, a very helpful woman pinned me so thoroughly inside of my ensemble, I looked like I was undergoing acupuncture. While I held my breath for a dangerously long stretch, she took my skirt over and up and by the time she was through with it, my cheap shoes from Payless peeked under the hem. Unfortunately, all of her needles and all of her pins couldn't make the top look like I would fit in. "Are you going to put boobs in that, dear?" she asked matter-of-factly as she scrutinized my appearance in the mirror before us.

"You mean besides the ones I already have in here?" But we both knew that my comeback was lacking. My endowments fell far short of filling out my attire. So again, let me assure you that I don't want to be your bridesmaid. I'm opposed to strapping on extra body parts when they have nothing to do with my own enjoyment.

This brings me to the night before— the night before the wedding. When I asked Dixie for directions to the rehearsal dinner, there was just one thing I'd managed to commit to memory. The wedding was in Chattanooga. The dinner, however, was at a restaurant in Nashville, and it turns out that the ceremony followed suit.

Look, I'm asking you nicely. Just how much is too much for you to put me through? Not only am I uncomfortable in these surroundings, I actually don't fit in what you've decided I should wear. Plus, I really don't know where you're going with this. I thought I did, but I was way off base. You're getting so serious. Isn't it time to admit that this just isn't working out? We could save ourselves a lot of heartache this way.

Of course, I'd be a fool to turn down a free meal. So what if I made it to the restaurant at the wrong hour? Doesn't it count that I showed up, eventually, and accidentally ordered so much sushi on Dixie's mother-in-law's tab that the wait staff thought I was a sumo wrestler until they came out and got a look at me.

I still don't want to be your bridesmaid, though. I realize at this point, you don't care what I want. But I feel almost like I've eaten something that isn't agreeing with me. You know the feeling I'm talking about. The one right before you make a run for it.

Oh, crap, I forgot to get a gift. But I pretended that I arrived empty-handed on purpose. I told Dixie I was waiting to find out if she really wanted something that she hadn't received. Of course, it was the day of the wedding by this time and for some strange reason she seemed preoccupied. While she visited the Smoky Mountains for her honeymoon, I visited target.com in search of her registry. And someone, whose face I never even saw, sent her a muffin pan and a (fill-in-the-blank other bake ware item) that I'm sure she liked, in beautiful wrapping with a thoughtful enclosure.

The thing to do now is just to let me off the hook. I'll give back the bouquet. Mark my name out of the program. I tried to be what you wanted, truly I did. But I'm not the bridesmaid you always dreamed of. I don't even know the groom's last name. I don't. I promise you with all of my heart.

# Wanna Go Out Sometime?

Do not cringe when you read the following word, dating. Well, what happened? Did you cringe anyway? Why? This is the twenty-first century. Haven't you gotten the hang of it yet? Tsk, tsk.

I have a suggestion for you. First, imagine being out with someone you think you might be interested in, could possibly become interested in, or should definitely be interested in, according to everyone who knows you. Now, take this quiz I've formulated to help you figure out where your interest really lies or stands (as the case may be). But don't expect me to help with your love life on a regular basis. There are many good reasons why I'm not your therapist. And don't pretend you don't read *Cosmo* when you think no one's around. I saw you. Of course, I was only making notes for my own quiz, really. I never read it when anyone's around either.

Which one of the following are you doing? A) Going out with someone you could call your date. B) Still telling people you're not sure if you're dating, followed by asking them if they think you are. C) Insisting you're just friends. D) Telling yourself that you're getting to know each other better and it doesn't matter how long that takes.

When you're out with the potentially special person in your life, should you A) Offer to pay. B) Expect your date to pay, that is, if you know if you have a date. C) Keep mentioning how you made a special trip to the ATM just so you could go dutch.

When the thought of kissing comes up, do you A) Decide that it's still too soon? B) Decide it's clearly too late? Or C) Decide to keep thinking about it because maybe you're just friends and friends aren't supposed to kiss friends anyway. Or are they?

When you're buying a greeting card do you choose from a slot marked A) Love? B) Love/Friendship? C) Humorous? Or D) Blank?

Stop in the name of love! Before you see that certain someone again without knowing if you're seeing her or if she's seeing you, I'm going to tell you something you really need to know.

You're going about this all wrong. Know how I can tell? You're mixing romance and dating. It's a sure sign of how crazy you're starting to get. The next thing you know, you'll be using cute names like Foofy and Lovenest and maybe even Sugarbritches. You'll be calling to say you're on your way over even though you have a key and you're not afraid to use it. You'll even start wearing each other's clothes.

Before I wind up in someone else's pants (not that there's anything wrong with that), I've rewritten the script for *The Dating Game*. Here's how to play. Go out with someone, or someones, and have a good time. That's it. That's really all you have to do.

Here are some helpful guidelines for choosing the others you're willing to play along with. Only date those you don't want to sleep with under any circumstances. Or date those who are absolutely unavailable, no matter what their gender happens to be. There's a special name for people in these categories. They're called friends. You don't have to keep up with any anniversaries this way. At most, you'll be snared into a sentimental conversation from time to time, going something like this. How long have we known each other? No, it can't be. How exactly do you think we met?

Date friends who have at least one major credit card. That way it doesn't matter if your card's maxed out. They'll cover you without demanding that you perform the Karma Sutra on them later, especially if you've already done that and that's why you're now friends.

Date married couples. This is a truly win-win situation when you think about it. Double the food, double the chances that someone can cover you, double the party invitations, and you even have a double shot at staying over in a guest room of your very own.

Date single people who're divorced, not looking for commitments, and going back to school. They're totally motivated to see dollar movies, plus they have video rental cards for all of the stores in town. They'll take one car without squeezing your hand meaningfully while they use it to shift gears. They'll even IHOP with you, willingly.

Date single people who just haven't found that certain someone and who know it's not you. You can languish through love's latest labors lost together. Not that either of you would've ever made a fool of yourself, of course. Just that you were dating someone really stupid who didn't know what a good thing she was letting get away, again.

Date people online. This is every bit as time consuming as regular dating only you can both be naked the entire time without ever having to look at each other.

So the next time you find yourself home alone, who you gonna call? Someone you have to entertain all night, hoping she won't call you angel of the morning? Or someone who'll fall asleep in front of the TV with you and make you breakfast the next morning without ever forcing you to meet her family?

See Foofy. See Foofy run. Run, Foofy, run.

# I Would've Gotten Away with It, Too...

"Oh, hi," said the girl from across the street. "Did you buy this house?"

"Yes, I did," I said.

"Did you know it's haunted?" she wanted to know.

"No. The realtor didn't tell me that."

"The man who used to live there, he died in the bathroom. But he was really nice anyway."

Maybe that's why the TV screen turned as red as blood after a storm knocked out the power. In fact, it turned as red as the hair on the girl across the street. And a guy who drives a van stops by there, to visit another guy who has a goatee. Plus, they have a dog who's afraid of his own shadow.

Jenkies, I think I've found a clue. If my life really was like a cartoon from the '70s, I'd put on a bad disguise, try to scare everyone away from my new place, and bribe the dog with Scooby snacks.

But none of the places that Shaggy and Scooby ever entered with their knees knocking together like castanets was really haunted. It was all in people's heads, just like the girl across the street.

That is, until Comcast kind of hooked up my cable TV. I requested an installation where there was no previous cable, and in days a crew showed up to not fulfill my need. Claiming they couldn't do a full hook-up because they didn't have enough cable with them, which sounds just preposterous enough to be plausible, they left me with a "partial" connection instead. A cable stretched from the back of my house, through my front yard, across the street, and up Samantha's utility pole.

What happened next is something even Comcast can't explain. One at a time, letters began appearing on my TV screen. Each time I turned it on, the letter had changed but it was always uppercase and always white, as though the program was sponsored by the letter "P," for instance. Sometimes it would move during the course of a show, first center screen, next upper left corner, and finally somewhere in the lower right. "Perhaps it's P for prosperity," my friend Patrice suggested one night.

But it seemed more like P for possessed by the morning I awoke to the blood-red screen. When I called a service rep, she asked a very important question. "What's your cable box connected to?" I stared across the street at the utility pole and parked beneath it, the mystery van. What indeed, I wondered. Could they be haunting my house, instead of debunking it?

A few nights later, I unlocked my door to discover a piercing sound somewhere inside. It was the kind of piercing that leads to wincing and crawling and bleeding ears, all in the time it takes to determine that the house alarm system has been activated.

Mysteriously activated, said the ADT rep when I called to inquire about the problem, after deciding that standing outside in an ongoing thunderstorm was preferable to being inside my home. "I wonder if any of your neighbors have lost their power too." As I looked across the street, my eyes came to rest on a now-familiar vehicle, the mystery van. A dog behind the window looked out at me. "It's possible," I told her. And indeed it was, but it wasn't supposed to work this way. I was supposed to be the haunter, not the hauntee.

Then came the day when BellSouth connected the rest of

my phone extensions, after I quit pretending I could install them myself. Off I went to work, with all the dial tones working. Back I came that night to the deafening roar of static from every receiver. The sound was practically paranormal in nature.

So I drove back to work and called a BellSouth rep, who asked if there was another number where she could reach me. "Oh, if only there was," I told her snidely. But I, who can short out a digital watch in the push of a button, had never foreseen that almost every frequency I use would be jammed the moment I called a new place home. Called, hah. I'd call that pretty funny.

"I wonder if any of your neighbors are having phone trouble?" the rep asked me. "Do you know if they are?"

"Well, I can't see any of them right now," I said, imagining the mystery van in its usual spot, "but I'm sure they're not."

I was wrong, though. Dead wrong, you could say. It turns out Shaggy and the gang had a problem so frightening it went beyond my wildest nightmare. "We have a poltergeist," Samantha told me the very next night. "It threw the coffeepot all the way across the kitchen."

Dear God, not the coffeepot. "Tell me it didn't break," I said, as I felt a shiver run up my spine. The lack of a working phone line seemed miniscule, compared to a threat to my caffeine intake.

"The coffeepot's fine," she told me, shrugging. "We're used to that stuff. It takes more than a poltergeist to get us going."

So what's my excuse, I wondered. And then I realized what I was doing wrong. I was giving away the power to haunt my own house. And I would've gotten away with it too, if it hadn't been for those meddling kids.

I'm the only one, according to Comcast, whose cable box had an alphabet demon housed inside. Just like I'm the only one, according to ADT, whose alarm can deafen the living, wake the dead, and still fail to alert them that anything is wrong. And

BellSouth says I'm the only one who's called to have her phone lines repaired the very same day they already were.

Rumor has it my magnetic field causes these quirks and running a spoon down my spine will reverse my polarity. So who's not scared to spoon me? Any takers?

# The Difference Between Boy Scouts and Girls

"I thought you said they have a wonderful selection," I complained to my friend Larry, as soon as he got back from lunch. "But they have only one wall of CDs."

"You mean at the library?"

"Yeah, the downtown branch, only one wall of books on CD."

"But they have two more walls."

"Where?"

"Where you weren't looking."

I know what you're thinking. If you don't know me, you're thinking I didn't ask anyone where the rest of the CDs were. I just assumed that there was only one wall.

But you're wrong. As anyone who knows me will tell you, I did ask. I got the wrong answer. I probably asked the wrong question and clearly I left with no idea where most of the CDs are kept.

However, I went up to the woman behind the counter (on the same floor where I found the few CDs). I asked if all the CDs were on the side wall and she said yes. As God is my witness, she told me that's the selection.

So let this be a lesson to you. Don't send me to find something. I'll come back without it. It can be easy to find, according to you. There can be a lot of it and you can tell me exactly where it is. But when I come back, I promise you I won't have it. What I'll have, instead, is a very good excuse for an even better reason. A former co-worker, Robin, once explained to me that I return empty-handed for one, simple reason. I look for things like a boy does, and that means fruitlessly.

Once I overheard a conversation from another of my former co-workers, Heather. Her boyfriend called her at work to say he had an emergency. He couldn't find the jelly anywhere in their entire apartment and he already had the peanut butter on the bread. "Look on the refrigerator door," she told him, but he insisted that he had already and it wasn't there. "Then look everywhere," she told him, shifting the phone to her shoulder. "It doesn't matter what I tell him," she said to me. "I know it's on the door, but he won't find it. He can never find what's right in front of him."

The question is why do I suffer from an affliction that's associated with the opposite gender? It's possible I could be missing a gene, I suppose. My X could be alone, without a kemo sabe to keep it company. But I think it's more likely that I've picked up a Y somewhere along the way. I've heard you have to be careful about that. Ys are entirely too easy to catch. If found in time, Ys can be treated and no one will ever even know you had one, but if a Y is left untreated too long it can lead to serious consequences, such as blindness, deafness, and the inability to distinguish good taste from bad (especially when it comes to interior décor).

I believe I must've picked up my Y in childhood. (I know that's early, but I'm an overachiever.) At Camp SkyWaMo, according to the counselors, I killed more tabletop fairies than any other Girl Scout, except for Ambrosia, who preferred the name Chipper, and, along with me, dressed like a boy on fifties night. The counselors said I put my elbows on the table way too much, causing the fairy genocide, but I know the truth. Boy vision can make you a fairy crusher, unless you learn a better way to use it. Then it can make you a really good Girl Scout.

So even though my obvious blindness continues in my thirty-something years, I don't think I should throw in the towel just yet. At my eye exam the other day, I could still see letters and numbers directly in front of me, even though one eye was completely covered after the doctor blew air on the other one.

Of course, there's nothing else to see at eye exams and she did say that there could be glasses in my future. But I think that's because I went in the wrong office first. It said Sears Optical on the door, which means having to do with eyes. I know that much. I sat there for at least a good ten minutes while people ahead of me got fitted for glasses. I'd like to say I started to wonder if another door might lead to an office for eye exams. But the truth is it never occurred to me. Instead, I looked at a multitude of glasses I didn't need to wear until the man working there redirected me.

In Macon, the next day, where I was speaking at a college, I told my host, Liana, she'd be able to find the Howard Johnson only by looking for its funky orange roof. (Of course, that would never help anyone in Knoxville.) The whole way in off the interstate, the only sign I saw said "lodge entrance," I told her. So the following morning when I drove out behind her, and noticed an exceptionally tall Howard Johnson sign pointed in the direction of I-75, it didn't surprise me. It just felt right.

I can read a map, but I hate asking for directions. Chances are I've already reached my destination. I can rewire a light socket, but I can't find a bulb to test it when I'm done, even if I took the bulb out so I could fix it in the first place. And if you come by for lunch, more likely than not, you'll have to tell me where the jelly is, unless you want a PB and B. But if you need help earning merit badges, aside from killing fairies, I'm here to tell you, I'm one hell of a Girl Scout.

# Duh Highlights

I did a dumb thing recently. I became a blond. It was an accident, I swear, the result of my friend Marla's home highlighting kit and my own stupidity about the effectiveness of an ingredient called bleach. But since I left my brunette roots behind, I've noticed something. I'm having more fun.

On a recent Sunday afternoon, I went on a trip with my friends Julie and Patrice to Joyce Kilmer Memorial Forest. It's just over the North Carolina state line, an easy drive from Knoxville along Highway 129, according to Patrice, who plotted our course. Only she'd never traveled 129 that far before and neither had Julie, who was driving the car.

In the backseat, I watched the scenery I know so well as it turned from the city of Maryville to Chilhowee Dam to the currently closed entrance of the Foothills Parkway to a section of the highway known as the Dragon. Beloved by motorcyclists far and wide, the Dragon is fourteen miles of roller coaster-style roadway where you'll swear you can see the back of your own vehicle coming around the curve you're currently on.

What it's not is a road to be traveled by the weak of stomach, and the brunettes up front were rolling down their windows even though we were being pummeled by rain.

"I want to know when this ends," Julie directed as the atlas landed in my lap.

But I was more interested in the sites outside the car. "Did you see that guy in the red and white leather?" I asked as the millionth motorcyclist revved from behind us to roar ahead, ignoring the double yellow line on the road. "His knee was practically on the pavement."

My front seat companions, however, were shut-mouthed and wide-eyed. I think their own knees may have inched closer to the pavement, judging by our speed as we crawled past the water-soaked greenery on the far side of the car and the sheer drop down the bluff just outside our passenger windows.

And then the road that had been pointing downhill suddenly started to climb again. "Why are we going up?" Patrice asked quietly, gripping the armrest extra tight.

But Julie had lost the last of her patience, though her lunch, amazingly, remained intact. "I thought we were going for a walk in the woods. I didn't know this was going to be a !@&*%*! endurance test."

At that moment, I realized a little-known secret of the universe. It's not easy being blond. Not only do you always have to have fun, it can't be just any fun. You have to have more fun than anyone else. The hair you wear is the cross you bear, so to speak. You have to overcome freak-outs, phobias, and a sure sense of doom. You have to chase all of your cares away because you're a blond, B-L-O-N-D even if you didn't mean to be one.

For those who haven't had highlights done at your friend's house, let me tell you a little something. It hurts like hell when someone forces a rubber skull cap onto your head and uses the equivalent of a crochet hook to yank your hair through a seemingly endless succession of very tiny holes that you can't see because you're convinced looking in the mirror would only make it hurt more.

And there are other reasons not to try this at home. You have to sit still and hold your breath while someone paints your still-hurting hair with a foul-smelling paste, then slaps a layer of Saran Wrap down tight over everything and sets a timer.

But probably the best reason is, because even after all of this, you may think you know better how it works than the person you trusted to do it for you in the first place.

Marla tried to get me to rinse my hair about fifteen minutes after the solution went to work. "No," I said, without looking at it. "My hair's darker than yours. It needs more time."

Now I ask myself, more time? I could've chosen to have my head slathered with foul-smelling paste for less time than I anticipated and if I decided that wasn't enough I could've said, "Marla, I'll just die if you don't pull my hair some more." I didn't do it, though. I wanted more. I wanted my hair to stink even more. I wanted to feel my forehead burn even longer as the solution decided to make a run for it. I wanted to listen to the crackling coming from the plastic on my hair while wondering if maybe I made a mistake. So at the end of my predetermined thirty-minute period, a somewhat startled, rather pissed-off and definitely lighter-headed version of me looked back from the mirror over Marla's bathroom sink.

I could've returned to my roots as a slightly phobic brunette with another home color kit and a timer set no longer than fifteen minutes, but that sounded like a sure way to not have fun. I'd never have gone bike riding for the first time in twenty years believing I wasn't destined to crash and die no matter how high the hills were or how fast I pedaled. And I wouldn't have canoed twenty-seven years after my last attempt, though my borrowed orange life vest felt more like a neck brace, instead of drowning repeatedly in my imagination without even setting foot near shore.

Unfortunately, my highlights have developed a dark side. That's right. My roots are showing. Does that mean my sense of fun will come screeching to a halt, like Julie's car at the end of the Dragon when she saw a sign for Tapoco Lodge? No way. I'll just march in demanding to know all the alternate routes and head to my destination.

# The Suck Factor

"Knoxville sucks!" a teenager told me the other day. Of course, she was looking at her second smashed car in less than six months. It happened on the night of her senior prom, but I doubt there's a picture of her wearing her formal, posing with the driver of the wrecker.

I can think of several non-wreck reasons to agree with Vicky. For instance, when I was canoeing recently with Kate, the smell of a dead cow in Fort Loudoun Lake came very close to making me hurl. I know that the mayor wants to spend $1 million to fix up the Sunsphere, but I'd rather he spend $1 million to knock it down. I think it's likely that in the very near future, the number of orange and white construction barrels will outnumber Vol athletes by a ratio of at least a gazillion to one. And even though I found lethal carrot remains in my refrigerator the other night, it's Knoxville's air that gets the worst national attention.

So why am I here, along with a few hundred thousand other residents? It's simple. Knoxville, like the Blob, sucks people in.

At EarthFest, I saw my friend Annalee. I doubt she'd know the Vols Head Football Coach Phil Fulmer if he hit her on prom night, but she was using an orange and white umbrella, while explaining that she didn't know how she got it. I remember when she moved here in 1998. She was just out of college, lacking any idea of what to do with her life, but her parents were moving here, so she figured, what the hell? Now she's running her own faux finishing business and her house has been on the North Knoxville Christmas tour.

Annalee and I met in the Fort Sanders neighborhood, when she came to the Laurel Theater on purpose. I believe that many people go into the Fort and don't come back out for several years. When I lived in the Fort for six years in the '80s, people who wanted to visit me often called to say my apartment obviously did not exist. I'd already given them specific directions. I'd even reassured them that several streets are laid out in numbered blocks. Yet they drove repeatedly by all the one-way signs, becoming hopelessly lost; only finding a pay phone. It was often the phone across from my apartment, located on the corner of Fourteenth Street. I'd walk onto my balcony and wave at them. They'd come up. We'd walk over to the IGA. And the next time they visited, we'd repeat the experience.

A visit to downtown can be much like the Fort, only there's less free parking. I know people who've lived in Knoxville almost twenty years who insist they find places downtown only by accident. And when they're able to drive back out, they wind up on I-40 wondering how they'll ever return to Market Square. The problems, again, are the one-way streets. They form blocks that aren't really shaped like squares and suddenly turn into bridges forcing drivers to cross the Tennessee River where Baptist Hospital waits for them. Some buildings, such as the City County Building, leave potential patrons with the idea that there's never a parking space out front. One of my friends said she wouldn't pick up an accident report unless she had at least one other person with her. That person could drive around and around the building while she ventured inside, trying to find the department that had processed her paperwork.

When my friend Jenny moved to Chattanooga in 1998, she swore that Knoxville "was the suckiest example of urban planning I've ever seen." Now she rents my downstairs room back in Knoxville's Lincoln Park. She said Chattanooga's greatness ended in the layout and for the last five years she was bored, bored, bored, and bored. She came back just in time to appreciate the renovations going on downtown. And just in time for the announcement from the Tennessee Department of Transportation that construction will shut down the most direct exits for drivers on I-40.

Jenny's main problem with Knoxville is that there aren't enough sidewalks, which makes more people drive because they don't want to catch the bus because there aren't enough sidewalks to stand on and wait. But the people who do wait for the bus are choking from some of the country's worst air, caused, in part, by all the traffic created by drivers who don't have a few thousand extra for hybrid cars. Hybrids might not cost so much, however, if only there were more sidewalks in Knoxville.

My friend Patrice arrived here in the late 90's to begin a job with Scripps Productions. She told me then she'd be here for only a year or two, tops. She was thinking she might work her way west to the coast. I didn't tell her that if she really thought she was going to leave Knoxville, she should take another job and move the very next day. I didn't tell her some of the reasons I like living here. In no time, she would find Italian food to die for, a growing list of coffee bars, an art house theater, a concert scene from Tori Amos to Gillian Welch to ZZ Top, and plenty of places by the river where her dog, Gus, could roll on dead fish. I did tell her that some people complained about the lack of sidewalks.

As I write this in the spring of 2004, Patrice just moved into a renovated downtown apartment after deciding she hasn't found a house she wants to buy and she has the same job she had when she arrived. She could move if she wanted to. She's had job offers stateside and overseas. But what she told me the other night is that she knows people here and she really likes that. Plus, Gus just loves to go to the Tennessee River. He thinks there's nothing like the dead fish in Knoxville.

I was sucked back to Knoxville from Miami in 1994. I could say it happened because my friend Allison asked me to help her start teaching etiquette for kids, but if you knew me you'd never believe that. What you should believe is that I could afford to live here and write while I worked retail till I got a real job. Throw in there that I love the Smoky Mountains, polluted as they are. I love the view from the hill at Lakeshore Park, although the grounds also house a hospital for people who've been committed. And I love my memories of the West Hills IHOP, when it was plastered with paintings of Jesus on the cross and a different waitress every week called me "honey."

Whenever your straw hits the bottom of your drink, someone else just moved to Knoxville.

# About the Author

Angie Vicars has a Master of Fine Arts in screenwriting from the University of Miami - although screenplays are what she writes least. She is a published columnist, poet, and online content writer-producer. Her first novel, *Treat,* was published by The Haworth Press, Inc., in 2001. She says that she is working on a second novel, but no one else has seen it.

In her spare time, Vicars likes to work on her house, read, watch movies, hike, drink wine, and enjoy time with her pets.